THE SECRET
OF CONFESSION

BOOKS BY
FATHER PAUL O'SULLIVAN, O.P.

HOW TO BE HAPPY—HOW TO BE HOLY

ALL ABOUT THE ANGELS

AN EASY WAY TO BECOME A SAINT

THE HOLY GHOST—OUR GREATEST FRIEND

READ ME OR RUE IT

HOW TO AVOID PURGATORY

THE SECRET OF CONFESSION
Including The Wonders of Confession

THE SECRET OF CONFESSION

Including

The Wonders Of Confession

by

Father Paul O'Sullivan, O.P.
(E. D. M.)

> *"Whose sins you shall forgive, they are forgiven them; and whose sins you shall retain, they are retained."*
> —John 20:22-23

TAN BOOKS AND PUBLISHERS, INC.
Rockford, Illinois 61105

CUM PERMISSU SUPERIORUM.

Imprimatur: Canon Emmanuel Anaquim, V.G.
                Lisbon
                October 15, 1936

First published around 1936 by Edições do Corpo Santo, Lisbon, Portugal. Retypeset and reprinted in 1992 by TAN Books and Publishers, Inc., with permission of Saint Martin de Porres Apostolate, Dublin, Ireland.

ISBN: 0-89555-459-3

Library of Congress Catalog Card No.: 92-61255

Printed and bound in the United States of America.

TAN BOOKS AND PUBLISHERS, INC.
P.O. Box 424
Rockford, Illinois 61105

1992

"The writer has conferred with many
experienced confessors,
and all, without exception,
agree that no vice is so gross,
so deep-rooted, so vicious
that it will not yield
to frequent Confession..."

(Page 93)

9 April 1943

Dear Father O'Sullivan,

I approve most heartily of your booklet on Confession. It supplies a need much felt, viz., a clear and practical explanation of the strength and consolation which Confession gives to the faithful.

You rightly emphasize the fact that Confession does not only pardon sin but that it efficaciously helps the greatest sinners to sin no more; it gives the weakest strength and consoles the most abandoned, if only they confess frequently.

You touch on points which are little understood, even by many Catholics, and your book will afford most interesting and useful reading, not only to Catholics, but also for those who do not belong to the Church.

Every chapter has an attractive title and grips the attention.

I have no doubt that the book will throw new light on the minds of many regarding the great Sacrament of Confession and exercise a beneficent influence even on non-Catholics.

With best wishes for the success of your book and with my cordial benediction,

✠ P. CIRIACI, *Apostolic Nuncio*

CONTENTS

Part I
THE SECRET OF CONFESSION

Part II
THE WONDERS OF CONFESSION

—Part I—

THE SECRET OF CONFESSION

Including

Confession Was Instituted by Christ.
What Protestants Think of Confession
Facts Are Stubborn Arguments
Why Does God Oblige Us to Confess?
All Men Need a Friend
The Choice of a Confessor

Chapter 1

WAS CONFESSION INTRODUCED BY A BISHOP?

At a fashionable reception in the metropolis [of Lisbon], a party of well-known Catholics was gathered together to pass a social evening.

Just as a distinguished foreigner was addressing a group of ladies and gentlemen, a friend of mine entered the room and overheard the following remark:

"Excuse me, Madam," said the stranger, "I did not exactly say that Confession was bad or evil, nor did I wish to imply that it was useless. I merely said that it was all very well for ladies, who, doubtless, find it very consoling to be able to unburden their consciences to a priest. But we men do not require such consolations!"

The lady thus addressed quickly replied: "And pray, Sir, how can men consider themselves dispensed from a law which was established for all? Don't men also have souls to save, and are they not, too, obliged to obey the commands of God?"

The stranger continued: "My dear Lady, the idea that Confession was instituted by God is an illusion. It was not God who instituted Confession;

it is a purely human invention. Where do we find
mention of it in the first ages of Christianity?
If it were of divine origin, of course the obligation to confess would also fall on us. Confession
was, as a matter of fact, instituted and introduced
first in Germany, in the fourteenth century, by
Bishop Fuller." And the stranger supplied, with
the utmost effrontery, names of places, dates, and
facts entirely fantastic.

On hearing this, the listeners were aghast. Some
made attempts to defend the doctrine of the
Church, but none of them was sufficiently
grounded in his or her religion to be able to refute
with authority the falsehoods of the distinguished
guest.

On the following day, the friend who had wit-
nessed the above incident called on me and,
regretfully admitting his inability to disprove the
stranger's statements, asked for full enlightenment
on the matter.

Now it seems to me that many Catholics, if they
found themselves in like circumstances, would
experience the same difficulty. True, they have a
certain *vague* knowledge that Confession was
instituted by Our Lord and practiced from the
earliest times, but were they asked for a proof,
they, like the Catholics just mentioned, could not
give a reason for their faith. Still less could they
explain — if challenged by a Protestant or
unbeliever — the sublime beauty, the divine
efficacy, the splendid results and the immense consolations of Confession. And least of all could

they answer the many difficulties so frequently urged against this great Sacrament.

To supply what we consider a great want, we venture to offer the public the following little work, which while showing that Confession was indeed instituted by Christ, will also show what a source of deep consolation and strength it is to those who understand it. Many Catholics never grasp the true idea of Confession, and some even find it a very painful and disagreeable duty.

Protestants, as a rule, find the idea repugnant, but strange to say, many among them, when once they hear it explained, feel a positive need of it, and it not infrequently hastens their entrance into the Catholic Church.

We flatter ourselves that both Catholics and Protestants will read our little book with keen interest and derive not a little profit from its perusal. It is popular in style and stresses several points of importance. The method is simple but attractive, and the reader becomes so engrossed that he is reluctant to put the book down until he has read the last page.

One of the special features of the little work is that it shows what an infinite source of consolation and help Confession is to the sorrowful and weak and what a powerful means it is of snatching boys and girls from the brink of some hidden danger. It also proves that, far from robbing a man of his manliness — as a distinguished Protestant statesman has rashly asserted —

auricular* Confession makes a man a brave soldier, a loyal citizen and a trusty friend.

---

*The term "auricular" refers to Confession made privately and "heard" by a priest.—*Editor,* 1992.

Chapter 2

CONFESSION WAS
INSTITUTED BY CHRIST

The Son of God came on earth to save man. From what? Clearly from sin and its consequences. All Christ did when on earth—the sublime lessons He taught, the admirable doctrine which He bequeathed us, the Sacraments He instituted, the miracles He worked, the law He promulgated, His precepts and counsels—*all* were destined for the great end of saving man from sin.

The 33 years Our Lord passed with us here below, His cruel sufferings, the Precious Blood He shed and His death on Calvary had for their one great aim to purge the world of sin. Had He not achieved that end, His mission would have been a failure.

It was for this object that He came. He loved sinners, lived with them and called them to Himself. One of them, **Peter,** a weak and sinful man, He made the head of His Church. **Paul,** a fierce and relentless persecutor, He made the Apostle of the Gentiles and a "vessel of election." **Magdalen,** an erring, sinful woman, the scandal of the city in which she lived, He chose for His special friend, made her a model for penitents, and even-

5

tually associated her with His Immaculate Mother.

If Our Lord's acts were not sufficient to clear away doubts on the subject, let us listen to His express declaration: "I am not come to call the just, but sinners." (*Matt.* 9:13).

Now, if Christ has given to His Church the power to continue His mission for all time, and guaranteed it His fullest protection—"Behold I am with you all days, even to the consummation of the world" (*Matt.* 28:20), "The gates of Hell shall not prevail against it" (*Matt.* 16:18)—it would be, indeed, a matter of surprise if He had not given to that Church an excellent and supreme remedy against sin, since He had come on earth expressly for this end, moved thereto by infinite pity, mercy, goodness and love.

Surely no one will doubt Our Lord's power to achieve what He so ardently desired, and still less call into question His boundless love and generosity. That omnipotent Power which drew the vast universe from nothing by a single word could find no difficulty in raising up His weak ones, forgiving them and confirming them in the path of justice. That same Love and Generosity which led Him to lay down His life in the midst of terrible torments would surely do all it could for those for whom He had died.

The means—the remedy Our Lord left against sin—is Confession, in which the sinner is not only pardoned of his guilt, but (mark it well, Dear Reader) receives strength and power to avoid sin for the future.

He says to each penitent who goes to Him in this Sacrament what He said long ago to the sinful woman: "Thy sins are forgiven thee, go in peace and sin no more." Not only does He *bid* penitents sin no more, but He gives them the *strength* and the *will* to sin no more.

HISTORY SPEAKS

All Christian peoples, and at all times, have held that Confession was instituted by Christ. So certain and unshaken was this belief that the Church was never called upon to publish in regard to the doctrine of Confession any of those numerous and dogmatic declarations or carefully worded explanations and definitions which she was obliged to publish regarding many other doctrines which were controverted or denied by heretics at one time or another.

It has frequently happened in the history of the Church that doctrines not yet defined have been freely discussed by theologians of different schools of thought until the moment when the Church thinks well to intervene. Then of course all discussions cease, according to the saying of **St. Augustine:** "Rome has spoken, the case is closed." [*Roma locuta est; causa finita est.*] But with regard to Confession, the opinion of theologians has always been unanimous. Infallible authority has never had to intervene.

WHAT THE HOLY FATIIERS SAY

St. Basil writes as follows: "Necessarily our sins must be confessed to those to whom has been committed the dispensation of the mysteries of God. It is written in the Acts of the Apostles: 'They confessed to the Apostles, by whom also they were baptized.'" (*In Rrg. Brev.,* q. 229, 2, 11, p. 492).

St. Ambrose: "The poison is sin, Confession is the accusation of one's crime; the poison is iniquity, Confession is the remedy against the relapse. But art thou ashamed? This shame will avail you little at the judgment seat of God. Overcome it at once."

St. Augustine: "Our merciful God wishes us to confess in this world that we may not be confounded in the other." (*Hom.* XX).

St. John Chrysostom: "We have reached the end of Lent. We must make a full and accurate Confession of our sins." (*Hom.* XXX). "To priests is given a power not given to Angels or Archangels, for Jesus says: 'Whose sins you shall forgive, they are forgiven. Whose sins you shall retain, they are retained.'"

St. Jerome: "With us the bishop or priest binds and looses for having heard, as is his duty, the various kinds of sin; he understands who should be bound and who should be loosed." (*Com. in Mth.*).

Reading the context of these Fathers, it is abundantly clear that they are speaking of auricular

Confession [i.e., Confession spoken privately to the priest, who *hears* it].

Thus the doctrine of Confession never raised any controversy. We find no mention of such in history, nor are documents relating to it preserved in libraries or archives, for the simple reason that no doubts ever existed regarding the Divine institution of auricular Confession.

Chapter 3

WHAT A STORM
WOULD HAVE ARISEN!

Moreover, were Confession an invention or idea of any given Pope, bishop or priest, or had it been imposed by any human authority as an obligation — still more as a Sacrament — what a storm of discussion, what angry disputes would not such an attempt have caused! When even questions of purely dogmatic nature gave rise to such bitter and lasting contention, what would not have happened if any man — bishop, priest or even Pope — had commanded men to confess their secret sins and crimes, their shameful weaknesses to other men, and if, on his own initiative, he had claimed that a simple man could be appointed by a man to pardon sin?

No mention of any such storm exists. None such ever arose, because **auricular Confession** came down to us from the dawn of Christianity as an essential part of the Law established by Christ.

Again, if Confession had been instituted or introduced by a bishop or Pope, our adversaries would surely be able to tell us who that Pope or bishop was; also, when it was introduced, and in what country! No such facts are mentioned in any history or given us by any writer. No one can point out a date when Confession was first practiced in one country and not yet in another. The truth is, it was practiced simultaneously by all Christians, at all times, and in all countries, wherever Christians existed.

HERETICS AND SCHISMATICS
ADMIT CONFESSION

There is another consideration worthy of mention. From the earliest times, bodies of Christians — schismatics and heretics — occupying extensive regions, and comprising whole races, fell away from obedience to the Church. These have always been bitterly hostile and ever ready to launch an attack on Mother Church, whenever a chance was forthcoming. Certain it is that they would never have accepted any such doctrine or institution as auricular Confession if it had not clearly come down from Christ Himself.

Now the fact is, these bodies of Christians not only accept the Divine institution of Confession, but are warmly attached to it, and practice it. If they did not receive it after their separation from Rome, they must always have had it, and from the early days.*

There is not the smallest evidence, therefore,

---

*The schismatics and heretics who accept the Divine institution of Confession would be chiefly the Orthodox and Anglicans. — *Editor,* 1992.

of the human institution of this Sacrament, but on the other hand, the clearest possible mention of Confession as of Divine institution is made by the early Fathers: St. Augustine, St. Jerome, St. John Chrysostom and a whole host of others, as we have already remarked.

We can trace the practice of Confession from our own day, going back century after century, to the times of the Apostles. We find not only women and children, but powerful monarchs, distinguished savants, brave soldiers, men of every stamp of character humbly confessing their sins and craving absolution. It is recounted of St. Ambrose, for instance, in the 4th century, that he used to shed tears when hearing Confessions and, by this example, soften the hearts of the most hardened sinners.

A FALSE ARGUMENT

History and Tradition are so clear and certain on this point, viz., that Confession is a Divine institution, that the enemies of Sacramental Confession are driven to the most ridiculous extremes to find an argument, however shadowy, in proof of their contention.

As a consequence, abandoning the myth of human institution, they have recourse to the argument that Christ Himself pardoned sin, and argue that therefore there was no reason to bestow such a power upon men!

It is manifestly true that Christ saved man by His Sacred Passion and at the price of His Precious Blood. But it is necessary that the merits of the Death and the Blood of Christ be continually **applied to each individual soul.** Our Saviour paid an infinite price for our Redemption; but, notwithstanding this glorious Redemption, we have not been transformed into angels, we are still weak mortals, we are still buffeted by temptation, we still stagger and fall. Sin still continues to exist and cause havoc in our midst. Men sin and remain in sin; they lie and steal and fall into the innumerable faults to which weak human nature is prone.

God left us our free will, that great faculty which makes us like to the Angels and even to Himself, and which He could not deprive us of without destroying our nature. But we most shamefully abuse this gift of liberty and, despite all God's goodness, continue to sin often and to sin grievously. Sin, unfortunately, abounds. God came to save us from sin. Surely, then, He must have given us an efficacious remedy to pardon sin, on the one hand, and on the other to give help and strength to avoid new falls. That remedy is manifestly **Confession**.

CHRIST INSTITUTES CONFESSION

The words in which the Sacred Scriptures relate the institution of Confession are so clear that there cannot be the slightest doubt about the matter. Before instituting the Sacrament, Our Lord had already promised it to St. Peter: "And I will give to thee the keys of the kingdom of Heaven. And whatsoever thou shalt bind upon earth, it shall be bound also in Heaven: and whatsoever thou shalt loose on earth, it shall be loosed also in Heaven." (*Matt.* 16:19).

He repeated the same promise later, this time to all His Apostles: "Amen I say to you, whatsoever you shall bind upon earth, shall be bound also in Heaven." (*Matt.* 18:18).

Finally, He instituted the great Sacrament itself, using words categorical and clear:

"As the Father hath sent Me, I also send you. . . Receive ye the Holy Ghost. Whose sins you shall forgive, they are forgiven them; and whose sins you shall retain, they are retained." (*John* 20:21-23).

Note these formal words: "As the Father hath sent Me, I also send you." Who, after this definite statement of Our Saviour, shall dare to doubt that He instituted Confession? Sacred Scripture later on gives us proofs of the exercise of this sacred ministry, for it is stated in the **Acts of the Apostles:** "And many of them that believed, came confessing and declaring their deeds." (*Acts* 19:18).

St. James in his epistle says: "Confess therefore your sins one to another: and pray one for another, that you may be saved." (*James* 5:16).

Chapter 4

WHAT PROTESTANTS THINK
OF CONFESSION

We frequently meet with Protestants who, though not themselves believers in Confession, still have very clear and accurate notions of its wonderful efficacy.

Some, too, have actually joined the Church because they desire to confess. We shall quote a few instances.

Half a century ago, when the hostility of many Protestants against Catholics had reached the point of fanaticism, a Dominican monastery was founded in a district of England where the vast majority of the inhabitants were Protestants, and the few Catholics existing there were mostly taken from the poorer classes.

The Protestant minister was a local magnate and did not condescend to manifest the smallest sympathy, much less friendship, for the poor friars who had come to settle in his parish.

The amazement, therefore, of the Superior of that monastery can well be imagined when one morning the Brother Porter announced that the Protestant clergyman, the Rev. Mr. Burton, wished to speak to him. He went at once to the parlor to ascertain the reason for the unexpected visit.

His smile of welcome was received by the visitor with cold reserve.

"I am not pleased with my servants," the clergyman began, "and I do not intend to pay them their wages."

"But, my dear Sir," objected Father Thomas, thoroughly taken by surprise, "what have I to do with your servants? Since, however, you honor me with your confidence, permit me to say that you do not act justly in refusing their wages to the poor people who serve you."

"I have not quite finished my explanation," returned the minister. "My servants are Catholics — but they do not go to Confession. Why, Sir, do you think that I keep Catholic servants in my house, instead of Protestants, as would be natural? It is because I wish them to go to Confession, for Confession, I hold, is a guarantee of their good behavior.

"If they go to Confession, I feel sure that they will not rob me nor talk badly of me, but will fulfill their obligations conscientiously. I know that the members of the Roman Church are obliged to confess all their sins, such as stealing, injustice, services badly performed and other like faults and defects. I am fully aware of the restraining power of Confession. That is the reason I keep Catholic servants in my house, but on the express condition that they go to Confession. If it were not for this I would not have come to disturb your Reverence. I beg you, therefore, to admonish them. They form part of your flock."

Without further parley, he took his leave.

Needless to add, Fr. Thomas did as he was requested and admonished the erring servants. These, no less than the good Father, were astonished at the unexpected action taken by their Protestant master.

This fact reminds us of the words of the Divine Master: "The children of this world are wiser in their generation than the children of light." (*Luke* 16:8).

The case which we have related is not by any means an isolated one. Several similar instances have been brought to our notice. It is no unusual occurrence that Protestants prefer Catholic servants in their households for the simple reason that they consider them more worthy of confidence. Many Protestants, too, place their children in the hands of Catholic teachers and send them to Catholic colleges for the same reason.

This mode of thinking is in sad contrast with that of some so-called Catholics, who refuse their servants the necessary time and permission to go to Confession, as if the time spent in going to Confession defrauded them of a certain amount of household service. When will they understand that the frequent use of the Sacraments by their dependents is the best guarantee they can have of good and faithful service?

WONDERS WILL NEVER CEASE

"The following fact is one of the most extraordinary of my life," said a well-known priest to me.

"A Catholic lady came to me one day and told me that a young Protestant named George Miller wished to be received into the Church in order to marry a Catholic and asked if I would mind baptizing him. I replied that to become a Catholic simply to marry was not a sufficient reason for changing one's religion, but added that she might introduce the applicant to me.

"Some days later, she brought the young man along and discreetly left us alone. Without beating about the bush, my young friend came at once to the point. 'I wish to marry Julia, and I am ready to become a Catholic.'

"'My dear young man,' I returned, 'the wish to marry Julia is not a reason for embracing Catholicity.'

"'Pardon,' he replied, 'I did not express myself well. It is not merely to marry Julia that I wish to become a Catholic.'

"'In that case you must have some other reasons. What are they? Are you discontented with the religion in which you were born and in which you were brought up, the religion of your parents and your friends? Or is it because you see something in our Church that attracts you? What is the reason? What motive draws you to us?'

"Evidently George was not prepared for categorical questions. He hesitated an instant, and then replied: 'I wish to become a Catholic in order to go to Confession.'

"'Now, my friend,' I returned, 'frankly that is an extraordinary reason. It is precisely because of Confession that many of your co-religionists fear to embrace the Catholic Faith. And you mean to tell me that you actually wish to become a Catholic in order to be able to confess?'

"George at once, with unmistakable sincerity, gave me his ideas on Confession in words so clear and convincing as would put to shame many Catholics. He had grasped the full significance of the Sacrament and clearly understood what peace, strength and consolation it must give if properly practiced.

"'My dear Father,' he concluded, 'I have many Catholic friends, and speaking frankly, I don't think that they are any better than I am, but they can count on helps and advantages that are denied to me. When they fall into any faults or feel themselves dragged into temptation, I understand that they can go to Confession. From what they tell me, the priest is everything kind and only too anxious to help them. In fact, I know that he pulled some of them out of awful scrapes. They told me afterwards that they should certainly have gone to the devil had it not been for him, and I am sure of it.

"'Please, Father, do not take it amiss if I tell you bluntly that I have no use for Catholics who don't practice their religion. They are a rotten lot. I suppose it is the case of *Corruptio optimi pessima*. ["The corruption of the best is the worst."]

"'Now is it any wonder that I should like to have a friend to whom to go in my troubles. You can see for yourself that, though I respect my father and mother and love them dearly, there are many things I could not easily tell them. I have some good friends, too, but a man's secrets are too sacred and intimate, sometimes too complex, to confide to anyone except a confessional priest, such as I understand him to be.'

"Needless to say, I was not only convinced of George's sincerity, but I was amazed to find this young Protestant with such a clear comprehension of Confession."

CONFESSION AND RESTITUTION

Another fact that impresses Protestants profoundly is that important sums of money are annually restored to rightful owners through the medium of Confession. It is not easy to say which is the greater, their joy or their surprise, when a Roman Catholic priest gives them a sum of money with these few words: "I beg to give you this sum of money, which was confided to me. It was taken from you, and I am asked to restore it."

A little time ago a merchant living in the South of Ireland told me that a priest from the North had sent him £200 with the message: "The amount enclosed is money which was taken from your father many years ago and which has now been placed in my hands to restore to you."

GREAT PROTESTANTS AND CONFESSION

The very founders of Protestantism wished at the outset of the Reformation to save Confession at any cost.

The following statement was made by **Luther** in his work, *The Babylonian Captivity:* "I would prefer to continue subject to the tyranny of the Pope than to abolish Confession."

Melancthon deplored in the bitterest terms the abolition of Confession and declared that it was necessary to re-establish it.

Henry VIII, before falling into his tremendous excesses, spoke thus of Confession in his book on the defense of the Sacraments: "If I had not read of the doctrine of Confession in the Sacred Scriptures or in the books of the Fathers of the Church, it would be sufficient for me to see how it has been practiced by all Christian peoples in every age to be convinced that it is not a human invention but a divine law."

Little by little, however, the reformers were compelled by their followers, who were impatient of the slightest restraint and who wished to give vent to their worst passions, to reject the doctrine and practice of Confession. Yet, even to this day, the more enlightened Protestants lament the want of this most consoling Sacrament.

Leibnitz, the illustrious Protestant philosopher,

speaking of Confession, affirms. "We cannot but
agree that the institution of Confession is worthy
of the divine wisdom and that the Christian Religion contains nothing more noble or beautiful.
The duty to confess contributes much, first of
all, to keep us from sin—above all if our hearts
have not already been hardened and perverted.
Secondly, it is a great consolation for those who
unfortunately fall, for it helps them to rise. For
this reason, I consider that a pious, grave and
prudent confessor is a powerful instrument of
God for the salvation of souls. By his counsels
he serves to mold our affections, he points out
our defects, and he warns us of occasions of sin.
He exhorts us to restore that which we may have
stolen, to repair injustices we may have committed; he resolves our doubts and consoles us when
we are depressed. In a word, he helps to cure,
or at least alleviate, the weakness of our souls.

"If, on earth, there is hardly anything to be
found superior to a faithful friend, what is to
be said of that person who is obliged by an invio-
late Sacrament of religion to keep our confidence
secret, to lend us his aid and to give us his
counsels."

This glorious testimony, written with full
deliberation by a celebrated Protestant divine,
should be meditated on by every serious thinker.

No wonder then that thousands and thousands
of sincere and advanced Protestants are in our
day trying to restore Confession in their churches.

Chapter 5

FACTS ARE STUBBORN ARGUMENTS

At the outbreak of the first Great War [World War I], there were only 33 Catholic chaplains in the British Army. These were quite sufficient for the needs of the moment, since the vast majority of the troops were Protestants, or at least non-Catholics.

Moreover, the Catholic soldiers, over and above the assistance of the 33 official chaplains, had full liberty to frequent the Catholic churches in the ports and towns where they were quartered, and the priests of the district had also free access to the barracks, or, as the case might be, to the battleships.

When war was declared and the army had rapidly swelled its numbers, the government, composed entirely of Protestants, increased the number of **Catholic chaplains** to 600! These chaplains were treated with the utmost consideration and got from the first the rank of Captain, with full pay, together with additional funds for their expenses. In due time and in accordance with merit, they were promoted to the rank of Major, Colonel and even General, with the corresponding emoluments. All objects necessary for Catholic worship, such as altars, vestments and sacred vessels, were generously supplied. In no other army, as far as we know, was such consideration shown to chaplains.

Thus we have the eloquent testimony of a staunchly Protestant government to the value of Confession and the Sacraments.

The 600 chaplains distinguished themselves so notably that thousands of Protestants, lost in admiration at their zeal and organization, loyally published their praises at the close of the war.

Some of the great London newspapers, too, notwithstanding their purely Protestant outlook, did not hesitate to declare that "the Catholic soldiers, encouraged by the presence and ministrations of their *Padres,* feared neither man nor devil and were ready to face every danger."

No difficulties prevented these heroic priests from ministering to their men, living, dying or dead. They were well repaid, for the soldiers, fortified with the Sacraments, knew no fear and performed feats of incredible bravery. A non-Catholic officer, amazed at their coolness, remarked: "Why, these fellows face death with a smile on their faces."

Their heroic confrères of the French army, the bravest of the brave, also won the golden opinions of both officers and men, and their splendid courage did much to instill new life and energy into soldiers already worn out by fatigue and by the length and rigors of the war.

A few incidents will show still better what a

power Confession was during that awful time.

A dying trooper, near the French lines, asked his Colonel to act as interpreter, since the only chaplain available was a French priest. He was assured that he could make his Confession with signs. But he insisted on telling *all* his sins. Seeing the ardent desire of the poor fellow, the good officer, who was a Protestant, listened to the man's Confession and translated it for the French priest, who gave him absolution. Nothing could equal the gratitude of the dying solider, who died a few moments after, as happy as a child.

The Colonel was deeply impressed, asked many questions and ended by becoming a Catholic before the close of the campaign. Many of his brother officers did likewise.

The Bishop of Amiens, having on one occasion visited and spoken with 5,000 wounded officers and soldiers, ascertained that only 10 out of the 5,000 had not confessed and communicated! Needless to say, these 5,000 soldiers belonged to various regiments and came from different parts of France, so that the incident gives us a fair idea of what went on in the rest of the army.

On the arrival of the first detachments of American soldiers, some British chaplains courteously offered their services to the new arrivals. Great was their joy on learning that all the men had been to Confession one or two weeks previously.

A Swiss Protestant journalist received permission to visit the advanced posts of the Allied Forces and was given ample opportunity to speak with the soldiers.

On his return home he published beautiful accounts of the chaplains. "Among the wonders of this awful war," he wrote, "one of the most extraordinary is the appearance of a new kind of hero, *the priest hero,* of whom too much cannot be said. He is the admiration of everyone and a wonderful help to the men."

In strange contrast was the conduct of many of the Protestant chaplains, who, though brave and eager to do their best for their flocks, had to confine their efforts to providing material comforts, such as tea, sugar, tobacco and festive entertainments for the men when they were resting behind the lines. They could do nothing else; they could give no Sacraments, no spiritual help. The Catholic priests did all they could in the way of material help, but their real work was giving spiritual aid, hearing Confessions, giving Extreme Unction and Holy Communion, saying Mass, and thereby giving life, joy and consolation to the soldiers, who were then ready to meet death at any moment.

One night at the mess, where all the officers but one were Protestants, one of these told a beautiful story of the Catholic chaplain and, turning to his Catholic colleague present, said: "Your priests are fine fellows, but I am damned if I see what our chaps are doing."

Another added: "You Catholics can afford to be brave; you know where you are going, you have confessed. Hang it if I know what's going to happen to me if I fall."

The South African War. A Catholic soldier was brought in dying. He asked for a chaplain. The nearest priest was in an encampment 200 miles away. The fact came to the notice of Field Marshal Lord Roberts, who at once ordered a train to go and fetch the priest. On the return journey the small party was ambushed by the Boers and had to surrender.

On hearing, however, that the British Commander-in-Chief had sent a train such a distance to fetch a priest for one dying trooper, they were astounded. Giving the salute, they wished the party God-speed.

The capture of a slave ship. Some years ago a British warship had orders to watch for slavers, which were said to be plying their barbarous trade on the African coast. One of these was sighted but, disregarding the signals to come to, managed to round a promontory and get into shallow water.

A launch was ordered to follow and, if possible, capture her. The command was given to a young lieutenant, who boarded the enemy ship under a hail of bullets. A desperate fight ensued with the crew, which was composed of fierce desperadoes. The young commander behaved with conspicuous bravery and succeeded against heavy odds in securing the prize.

On his return to England he was rewarded with a captaincy. Replying to a speech at his old school, he said: "Gentlemen, I scarcely merit the praise you bestow on me. Though aware of my danger, I can't say that I felt any fear. I was at Confession a few days before and knew that I was alright."

Chapter 6

WHY DOES GOD OBLIGE US TO CONFESS OUR SINS TO A MAN?

The Son of God became man in order to be like us, and thus the more naturally to win our affections, gain our sympathy and compel our love.

As our Lord and Master He could have obliged us to serve and obey Him, but He chose rather, with ineffable goodness, to captivate our hearts with the sweet attractions of His Love.

His goodness, His sweetness, His tender affection, His mercy, His untiring patience, all reveal in a wonderful way His infinite Love. His Law is a law of love; His religion is a foretaste of Paradise. His two great precepts are to love Him with all our heart and to love our neighbor as ourselves.

If, therefore, our dear Lord gave us a religion of such sweetness and love, why does He impose on us the stern duty, the humiliating obligation of confessing our sins to men who are weak and sinful like ourselves? Did He not say to **Magdalen:** "Thy sins are forgiven thee, go in peace"? (Cf. *Luke* 7:48, 50). Why does He not address to each one of us like words of mercy and love? Why must we confess to a man?

When one describes Confession as a stern duty,

a humiliating obligation, he shows how little he knows of Confession. In plain truth, our Divine Master, when instituting the Sacrament of Confession, had in mind to give us profound and abiding **consolation,** not the wish to humiliate and shame us. After the Holy Eucharist, in which He gives us Himself, He has given us no greater benefit, no holier gift, no greater joy than Sacramental Confession.

We shall explain with all truth and clearness Our Lord's thought regarding Confession.

THE TEN LEPERS

When on earth Our Lord went about preaching His sublime doctrines, captivating all hearts by His boundless goodness, curing the sick, comforting the sorrowful, doing good to all. The multitudes were enraptured at His graciousness; their hearts burned within them when He spoke.

One day ten poor lepers called out to Him from afar off, for the Law forbade them to come nearer: "Jesus, master, have mercy on us!" They besought Him to cure them.

Jesus answered: "Go, show yourselves to the priests." (*Luke* 17:14).

He could easily have cured them without the intervention of anyone. Why did He send them to the priests?

THE RAVENING WOLF

Again, **St. Paul,** before his conversion, went about like a ravening wolf, persecuting the Church of Christ, possessed of the one idea of destroying the work of the Divine Master.

In pursuance of this impious project, he was actually on the road to Damascus, armed with authority to arrest and punish the followers of the Saviour, when Jesus spoke to him in words of inexpressible tenderness: "Saul, Saul, why persecutest thou me?"

The words pierced the heart of the fierce persecutor and changed the wolf into a lamb, hatred into love, the persecutor into the Apostle.

Trembling and repentant, Paul humbly asked: "Lord, what wilt thou have me to do?"

Our Lord answered: "Arise, and go into the city, and there it shall be told thee what thou must do."

Jesus was speaking to Paul; He could have told him personally what He wished him to do, or could have filled his soul with light and made manifest His will. But no, He sent him to Ananias, to His minister.

OUR RELIGION IS HUMAN AND DIVINE

But why stress so emphatically the fact that Jesus could pardon sins without Confession, that He could dispense in this matter with all human intervention, when the same point can be made in regard to all His relations with us.

Why pray to God! Does not God know all our
needs; is He not aware of what we wish and hope
for? Why does He, therefore, oblige us to ask, to
pray?

Again, could He not purify us from Original
Sin by one word? Why does He oblige us to be
baptized, to have water poured on our heads and
certain words repeated in the process, telling us
that, if this rite is not carried out, we cannot enter
Heaven?

Why is the dying man anointed with oil; why
do bread and wine have to be used in the Sacrament of the Eucharist? God could do all without
human intervention, without the use of material
things. Why did Jesus Himself use clay and spit-
tle when curing the blind man?

Our Catholic Religion is divine and human.
It is divine in its origin, in the graces it bestows,
in the lights, the peace, the consolation it gives.
It is human because it must be in conformity with
the condition of our nature, and in every way
adapted to our needs. God acts harmoniously in
all His works — *Omnia disponit suaviter* ("He arranges
all things delightfully") — but never so much as
when framing for us a most perfect religion.

A religion for men ought not to be cold or
abstract, neither should it be harsh or disagreeable, nor should it jar on our feelings, nor be at
variance with our sentiments and ideas. It ought
to correspond with the general laws of our being;
it ought to be perceptible to our senses, visible
and tangible. We act and derive our knowledge

through our sight, hearing, feeling, by the aid of imagination, memory and will. Our religion, in every way so important to us, should come within the range and fall within the grasp of our faculties. It should be a religion for human beings, not for angels; for weak and wayward sinners who need comfort, strength and pity, not for the Saints of Heaven.

Our Lord when preaching used language that was sublime but simple. He used examples and metaphors plain and suitable to His listeners, taken from the surroundings they were most accustomed to. In His comparisons He spoke of the flowers, the fields, the sea. The Kingdom of Heaven with all its glory He likened to a mustard seed. Himself He compared to a hen gathering her chickens under her wings.

In His dealings with the people, He stooped to the needs of the humble and sorrowful. With what divine condescension did He not console the poor widow of Naim when He raised her son to life; how affectionately He wept at the death of Lazarus; how lovingly He defended Magdalen when she knelt at His feet in the house of the Pharisee. How gently, too, He pardoned the poor woman taken in sin, how sweetly He bade the little children to come unto Him, and with what loving condescension He allowed John to rest his head on His divine bosom!

He became man in the truest, most complete sense of the word, sharing our feelings, our sentiments, our sorrows, susceptible to the same pains and subject to the same conditions of hunger, cold and weariness. He wished to be like us in every way so that we could more easily become like to Him.

For this identical reason, He wished to give us a religion suitable to us in every way: easy, natural, full of peace and consolation. We shall apply this doctrine to Confession in the following chapter.

Chapter 7

"COME TO ME, ALL YOU WHO LABOR AND ARE HEAVILY BURDENED."

In the Confessional the priest is the plenipotentiary of Jesus. He is there to continue the mission of Our Lord to sinners; he is there to dispense with the utmost generosity the mercies of God to men.

"O GOD, HAVE PITY ON ME, A SINNER."

The poor **sinner** laden with many sins, conscious of his failings and weakness, kneels at the feet of God's minister. He confesses his faults, many and dark though they may have been; he rises up pardoned.

His heart was full of pain and sorrow and shame, his conscience torn with remorse, his soul troubled with doubts and fears. He lays down this heavy burden at the feet of the priest; his sins are swallowed up in the abyss of God's mercy; he feels as though a mountain had been lifted from his shoulders. He faces life again with all its sorrows and temptations, feeling within himself a new strength, a new peace, a new life.

And the **priest?** He has infinite compassion for

the poor sinner at his feet. With what gentleness he helps him to confess; how lovingly he encourages him, how wisely he admonishes him, how humbly he makes the sinner feel that he, too, is a sinner and weak. Never for an instant does he feel disgust on hearing the sins of his penitent, no matter how grievous they may be; he does not despise him for the petty meannesses, the poor frailties, the violent temptations he may have to confess. In his inmost soul he thanks God for the grace of being able to save an erring soul. His is an immense consolation impossible to describe.

The **greatest and happiest moments** in the life of a priest are on the **Altar** with his God and in the **Confessional** with his penitents.

God implants in his heart a love and affection for the poor souls that come to him, akin to the love He implants in the heart of a mother for her children.

THE LITTLE CHILD

If the penitent is a little child, innocent, pure and guileless, who has not yet felt the pangs of sorrow, nor been exposed to the keen blast of temptation, the work of the priest is, indeed, most delicate. He feels that "of such is the Kingdom of God," and how dear they are to the Master. He knows, too, how he will have to answer to the Angel of that child for the soul entrusted to his care.

Like a mother, he listens to the story of the

little faults and failings. He strives to guide the
faltering steps, to instill into the childish mind
loving thoughts of the dear God above, the beauty
of His service, the ingratitude of sin, the malice
of offending so good a Lord.

Thus the little seed is sown, the plant springs
up and God sees another spotless lily blooming
in His Garden.

A BROKEN HEART

The sweet child's face disappears and a sad one
comes to take its place. The priest now finds himself listening to the chastened voice of one in
deep sorrow, a poor soul tortured with doubt,
crushed with a weight of care, fighting against
a pain almost too bitter to bear.

He listens with bated breath to the sad story
of a broken heart, of blighted hopes, of a ruined
life.

What can he say, what words can he frame to
soothe that grief? He breathes a prayer to the
Spirit above, a quick, fervent call for help to save,
to comfort the sufferer at his feet; and the Holy
Spirit, the Comforter, whispers in his ear the needful message, the sage counsel, the words of mercy
that, like heavenly dew, fall on the soul of the
sorrowing penitent, giving comfort and courage
and the resolve to bear lovingly the Cross with
Christ who bore so much for us. The Cross is
heavy, but now she has received the strength to
carry it. Life is fast slipping away, and the doors

of the Eternal Heaven are opening. Those words of her ghostly friend have told her of **the reward surpassing great** that awaits her and of the never-ending bliss in store for her, where sorrow and grief shall be no more.

Long, weary hours, day after day, for many succeeding years, the priest labors in the Confessional. He listens, he pardons, he comforts, he encourages, he raises up, ever snatching souls from Hell and presenting them to God.

This is the Confession that some benighted Protestants fail to understand and that even some foolish Catholics think hard and disagreeable.

What, we ask, could be more human, more helpful, more consoling? What more worthy of God's sweetness, mercy and love!

Chapter 8

ALL MEN NEED A FRIEND

What is it that we all desire when fear or doubt, sorrow or misfortune finds us out? Surely it is a friend, a true, a loyal, a prudent, a loving friend to whom we can pour out our grief, from whom we can seek advice, who will sympathize with us and console us.

There is an instinct embedded in our natures which moves us to seek a friend when in trouble, to unburden our heart of the weight that crushes it. Essentially social, we must willingly share our joys and our sorrows, our fears and our hopes with others. The mother consoles her children as none other can do; the gentle, sagacious wife comforts her husband when the brunt of sorrow pains and disappoints him; and a friend is never so much a friend as in the day of tribulation.

So Jesus, who knows us as no other knows us, says: "Come to me, all you that labor, and are burdened, and I will refresh you." (*Matt.* 11:28). This is His idea of Confession.

He appoints His priest to represent Him, to be another Christ. He bestows plenary powers on this delegate, assists him with divine inspirations, and prepares him with many years of study—all of which fit him for the great ministry He calls him to.

PERSIANS, CHINESE AND JAPANESE CONFESS

Every human being, no matter what his race or temperament, be he Christian, Jew or pagan, feels this need of someone to whom he can open his heart. So true is this that the Hindus, the Persians, the Chinese and many other pagan peoples have actually instituted a kind of "Confession" of their own, to supply this pressing demand of nature.

Unfortunately, their "Confession" is far from perfect, lacking, as it does, the divine helps and guarantees, the graces and consolations which God alone can bestow—and above all, the absolution of the priest. Yet their humble effort is productive of great good and has often very palpable results. The move is in the right direction, though the guarantees are lacking.

MORTAL SIN

We all feel the torment caused by a thorn embedded in our flesh. In fact, any substance foreign to our being causes us pain, and we never rest until we extract it.

Far and away more serious is the poison which sin pours into our souls. Bitter remorse, the fear of punishment, the consciousness of God's anger weigh us down and oppress us.

When in **grievous sin,** we are in open revolt against God. If by any chance the slender string of life should snap, we would fall into Hell without the faintest hope of escape or pardon. As long as we continue in this awful state, we are in the power of the devil. We have driven God from our sides, we are His enemies and in conflict with Him. As a consequence, the Evil Spirit holds a mastery over us and strives in every way in his power to injure us, to annoy us, to ruin us.

Who could possibly sleep in peace with a viper in his bed? Who would consent to sleep with a raving lunatic in his room? Who would dream of handing himself over to a cruel or relentless foe? Yet this is what those men and women do who commit mortal sin and remain in it.

No one would accuse the Angelic Doctor, St. Thomas Aquinas, of useless fears or exaggerated scruples. Yet he declares that not for all this world would he rest one night in the state of mortal sin, nor could he understand how any man with the use of reason could dare to do so. The danger of death is always imminent, and "It is a fearful thing to fall into the hands of the living God." (*Heb.* 10:31).

CRIMINALS CONFESS THEIR CRIMES

It is a well-known fact in the chronicles of crime that men who have perpetrated some awful crime and who succeed in escaping from the hand of justice are never at rest. The vision of their sin,

the face and the blood of their murdered victim
is ever before their eyes. A strange fear haunts
them day and night, their lives become a perfect
hell.

Finally, no longer able to bear the dreadful torture, they voluntarily confess their crime and hand
themselves over to justice. Perpetual imprisonment
in the severest penal settlements, or even the disgraceful death of the scaffold comes as a relief
from the torture of a bad conscience. If these
unfortunate men had only had faith, and could
have gone to the feet of Christ's representative
and confessed their sin, they would have found
relief in His pardon and in their own repentance.

Judas, after betraying Jesus, hanged himself in
despair. Had he gone to the feet of the Master,
or even made one act of perfect contrition, he
would have escaped his sad fate. Peter, who thrice
denied his Lord, repented, begged for mercy and
became Christ's Vicar on earth and now holds
the keys of the Kingdom of Heaven.

Chapter 9

THE CHOICE OF A CONFESSOR

We all have our individual tastes and likings and naturally choose our friends in accordance with these tastes.

God, too, in His gentle care of us, allows each one to select his own confessor.

Our parish priest baptizes and marries us; it is his duty, also, to administer the Holy Viaticum at the hour of death; but all are free to choose their confessor from among the many priests approved for Confessions.

Why is this liberty given us? That we may be perfectly at our ease when confessing.

Confessors have the rigorous obligation of treating with the utmost charity those who approach them, but like ordinary mortals, they have different temperaments, characters and manners, different culture and ideas. It is for the penitent to choose which he will.

Confessors do not act on their own initiative, nor do they base their decisions on personal opinions. They teach the doctrine of Jesus Christ, instill His counsels into the hearts of the faithful and make their decisions on principles laid down by Doctors of the Church. Thus their penitents have every guarantee of receiving sound doctrine and good advice.*

But in some things the confessor has to use his own discretion and judgment in treating with the weak and the strong, with the cheerful and the despondent, with the lax and the more devout. Some he stimulates, others he restrains, some he chides and others he consoles, for different diseases call for different remedies. What is food for one may be poison for another.

Again, the penitent has to choose the spiritual guide whom he understands best and who understands him best.

All should pray long and fervently to God to give them a spiritual father suitable to their requirements. It is incredible what progress one makes and what solid comfort one enjoys when in the hands of a competent guide. The gift of a good confessor is without doubt one of God's greatest graces. One Confession well made may change the trend of our whole lives, and many such Confessions are sure to do so.

Having found the Father and friend who suits us, we should not easily change for another. No one who has absolute confidence in his doctor

---

*Today, when many priests cannot be counted on to base their advice upon sound Catholic doctrine, the case is unfortunately often otherwise in practice. Fr. O'Sullivan's words about choosing a confessor in accord with one's own personal taste are of course based on the premise that all priests will give sound Catholic advice, which was the case at the time he wrote this book.—*Editor,* 1992.

cares to consult a stranger.

The custom of frequently changing confessors, or of going to the first at hand, is not recommended, for just as having many doctors may kill a patient, so also having many confessors may confuse a penitent. All doubtless give sound advice, but advice, like medicine, must be administered with method and judgment. If one frequently changes his confessor, how is it possible that the new one can understand his character and needs?

It is natural, too, that a confessor will give special care and use keener diligence to sanctify the souls that place reliance on him. He prays for them in Holy Mass; he watches over their progress and is encouraged by their efforts. He looks on them as given to him by God, his own children, his joy and his crown: *gloria mea et corona mea* ("my glory and my crown."—St. Paul).

There are confessors for all tastes, classes and degrees of culture. The parish priest is much sought after by his people. He is their Pastor and Father in Christ. He baptized and married them, shared their joys and their sorrows—and how many has he not accompanied to their last home in the quiet graveyard. He has many claims on them, and well they know it.

Many professional men, doctors and lawyers, scientists too, and journalists seek out a learned Dominican versed in the doctrines of St. Thomas to inform themselves the better on the problems presented by their professions.

Good Fr. Anthony, down at St. Francis' Priory, has his Confessional surrounded by his beloved poor, who venerate him greatly.

At Holy Name, many like the breezy manner and the masterful way of Fr. Stanislaus, who seems to push them on in the way of salvation. Others prefer dear Fr. Ignatius, whose culture and graciousness draw round him crowds of the elite.

Then there is Fr. Berkley at Old Mills with 500 scouts, the finest body of stalwarts in the county. He is eclipsed only by Fr. Dominic, turned 30 last birthday, who seems to be a veritable old Grandfather in the midst of his 200 catechism tots, varying from irresponsible seven-year-olds to mature fourteen-year-olds. One would think that they would tear him to pieces with their endearments.

In the country parishes there is no one like the young curate, whom the people say—and of course they know it—will be the next Bishop. At a moment's notice he is making his way across the bog-land or climbing the mountainside to take Viaticum to the dying, and it does not matter in the least if it is winter or summer, day or night. The sick call is God's call, and no priest would dare to hesitate when it is a question of saving a soul. If through his fault a single soul were to slip away without the Sacraments, what a lifelong remorse! How many priests die victims of duty, drenched to the skin on a bleak winter's night taking Viaticum to a dying penitent, or caught by the fatal typhus when absolving the sick laborer in his poor little cabin. Glorious martyrs of Charity!

On Sundays he is in the midst of the boys, preparing for the football match, as enthusiastic as the youngest, recommending a warm welcome and kind courtesy for the outsiders.

What truly wonderful men are these Catholic priests, and what a power is Confession!

— Part II —

THE WONDERS
OF CONFESSION

Including

Chapter 10

CARDINAL MERMILLOD
AND THE ACTRESS

The following story, told us by Cardinal Mermillod, is a beautiful illustration of what Confession really can do. The fact happened to the Cardinal himself and is one of the thousands of such incidents that are daily occurring and which give priests the most intense consolation.

His Eminence was at the time a simple priest, active, bright and keenly intelligent. He was heart and soul into his work; with him there were no half measures. Duty was not only sacred, it was a passion. There were very few priests in Geneva at that time; the duties of the mission were onerous and the atmosphere distinctly hostile.

One evening—it was rather late and he was tired, the day had been a busy one—a loud rap called him to the door. A young man, well-dressed and of prepossessing manner, entered and told him that his ministrations were needed. A lady was in danger of death. In reply to his inquiry whether the case were urgent, the messenger said that the case was grave and that he was requested to call the next day at that same hour. The house was distant and in a district little known to **Fr.**

Mermillod, who, therefore, carefully took note of the address.

Mindful of his promise, he made his way on the following evening to the home of the sick lady, which he found without much difficulty. It was a beautiful chalet in the midst of a garden and commanding a magnificent view of Lake Geneva.

He opened the gate and approached the house, noting that a dinner party was in progress, the dining room was alight, and that through the windows, which were open, the sounds of gay voices and laughter could be distinctly heard.

Somewhat mystified, he rang at the door, which was promptly thrown open by a liveried footman. On inquiring for the sick person, he was told that there was nobody ill in the house and that probably he had been given a wrong address.

"But is this not Chalet Violet and are we not in Rue Valois?" he asked, showing the carefully written address.

"The address is quite correct, Sir, but there must be a misunderstanding of some kind. There is no one ill in the house, and I cannot understand how a message should have been sent without my knowledge. It is my duty to see that such communications are delivered, and I receive corresponding instructions as to whom I am to receive."

"Might I speak with your Mistress?" suggested Fr. Mermillod.

"I regret, Reverend Sir, that my Mistress is at

the moment entertaining a company from the Opera at dinner, but if you insist, I will take her your message."

"I should be obliged if you did so since the case seems mysterious and I cannot easily come such a long distance again."

On hearing about the strange incident, the lady was naturally surprised and, telling her guests what had happened, suggested to her husband that it might be well to see the priest. Her husband accordingly went to interview the visitor.

"We are very sorry, dear Sir, to hear that someone without our knowledge has asked you to call. We cannot imagine who it could have been, or what could have been the motive of such an ill-timed joke.

"There is no one ill in the house, we do not belong to your religion, and just now we are entertaining some friends from the theater. Would you mind joining us at dinner? You are most welcome, and my wife will be glad to hear all about this singular incident from your own lips. Some of our guests, too, I believe, are Catholics."

Fr. Mermillod's first thought was to decline the invitation, but foreseeing the possibility of doing some good, he replied that he had already dined but would be glad to join the party.

After a brief word of introduction to the gay company, he was invited to take his seat near the hostess.

THE DINNER PARTY

"I have never had the pleasure of meeting you, Father," she said, "but we have all heard of you. We are, I am sure, delighted to have you amongst us, but what a weird experience! What was your visitor like?"

Fr. Mermillod described accurately the appearance of the young man who had called on him the previous evening—the last person, he should have thought, to perpetrate a practical joke—and repeated as nearly as possible the words his visitor had used, showing at the same time the address and the few words of instruction as to how to find the house.

"You Catholic priests must have strange experiences. Must you go to everyone who calls you, even if you don't happen to know them?"

"Yes, Madam, it is our custom to go to everyone who sends for us, if they need our ministrations."

"But have you many such experiences as the one of tonight?"

"We have, so to speak, **all kinds of adventures,** and meet with people of every description, but thank God we can do a great deal of good and bring untold comfort to many a breaking heart. I confess that I never had such an experience as that of tonight, but some of my colleagues have had cases quite as strange."

"Do please tell us, Father, of some of what you call your 'adventures.'"

Fr. Mermillod wished for nothing better and proceeded to tell some thrilling little episodes of his life. He was listened to with eager attention and plied with many pertinent questions, which were the best indication of the interest he had awakened.

With the delightful frankness that characterizes theater-going people, so different from the stiff ceremony and decorum of ordinary society, this body of actors and actresses manifested the greatest curiosity in hearing all he had to tell them. It was the first time that they had met a priest, and he was decidedly different from all their preconceived notions of clerics. He frankly surprised them by telling them of the wonderful thing Confession was, not indeed in so many words, but by the anecdotes he related. It was so utterly at variance with all they had heard or read before. His was really first-hand information; his patent sincerity gave his stories the ring of truth; and what he told them was all so human and sincere that it went straight to their hearts.

He had some good stories, too, of distinguished freethinkers with whom he had crossed lances, and of their ludicrous ideas of the doctrines of the Catholic Church.

Nothing, however, aroused so much interest as Confession, and about that they wanted to know everything.

One of the young actresses laughingly remarked: "How I should like to spend a few hours in the

Confessional and hear all the peccadilloes of my dear sisters."

The sally was greeted with a ripple of laughter all round.

"Ah, my dear Lady, though living in the midst of a frivolous world, I venture to say that you know very little of all its horrors and heartbreaks. Sitting in my Confessional for hours and hours at a time is, I assure you, a labor of **unthinkable sadness and weariness,** but a labor that is lightened by its own **consolations**.

"There we hear much that is beautiful and consoling, but there, too, we have to listen to heart-rending stories that make one almost sick with grief. Men and women of all classes, rich and poor, old and young, come and pour out to us the inmost secrets of their hearts, poor hearts so disillusioned and disappointed, torn and lacerated with a grief that cannot be described, with bitterness that has no remedy, with wrongs that cannot be redressed."

Turning to the window, he pointed to a pleasure boat on the lake with hundreds of tourists on board and said to the young actress: "You know what drives that boat with such speed through the waters? Steam pressure, is it not? Yet that very pressure might easily send the steamer and all its occupants to the bottom, were there not something in the mechanism to prevent such a catastrophe. That little something is the safety valve. When the steam pressure in the boiler reaches the almost bursting point, the safety valve auto-

matically lets off the excessive steam, and the pleasure boat goes on its way in perfect safety.

"The human heart is a boiler. It can bear great
pressure, but a point is reached when it can bear
no more. Grief, sorrow, constant care, ceaseless
worry, prove too much for human endurance. The
load is too heavy for frail nature to bear. We must
have relief.

"Confession is the safety valve. There the broken heart finds a balsam that soothes and comforts it; there the weak and faltering receive energy
and strength; doubts are chased away, fears are
put at rest, the most oppressed receive comfort,
black despair is dissipated and the bright light
of hope once more cheers the drooping spirit
that had well-nigh succumbed beneath the weight
of woe."

OBJECTIONS FROM THE DINNER GUESTS

"But dear Sir," ventured one of the company,
"don't you think that, instead of devoting so much
time to Confession, it would be better to amelio-
rate the lot of the poor, to improve material conditions, to educate and uplift the masses? Poverty,
misery and the consequent ignorance seem to me
to be one of the main causes of crime. After all,
the essence of Christ's law is charity."

"While giving attention to one set of evils, we
do not neglect the others," rejoined Fr. Mermillod.

"Have you no idea of the countless religious
orders whose members dedicate themselves whole-

heartedly to the poor, the sick, the ignorant, the
young and the old?

"Some receive in their institutions the aged of
both sexes and give them comfortable lodging,
good food and the most loving care. These are
the Little Sisters of the Poor.

"Others establish orphanages, where they pre-
pare boys and girls for the battle of life. While
instilling into their minds sound moral principles in the hope of making them good husbands
and wives, they teach them a trade or give them
a profession to enable them to gain an honest
livelihood.

"Some orders visit the poor in their own homes
and do all that God's sweet charity impels them
to for the relief of the indigent.

"There are hospitals and asylums for every possible need. Who has not heard of the Sisters of
Charity? Nothing, dear Sir, is left undone by the
Catholic Church to help the poor, but the greatest
work of all is **Confession, Christ's own blessed
work.** *'I am not come to call the just, but sinners.'* (*Matt.*
9:13).

"You will agree with me that moral suffering
is far and away the most terrible and the most
prevalent of human evils and one that threatens
the individual, the family, society and the country at large. It touches all classes, ages and
conditions.

"Crime in all its hideous forms, moral degradation, unbridled human passion, is what we aim
at uprooting and destroying by Confession.

"Can you point to any such institution outside the Catholic Church?

"You have police, courts of law, prisons, punishment—all, doubtless, needful. But we uplift criminals without punishment; we apply remedies that they accept joyfully; we do not compel them to come to us: they come of their own free will. They come saddened and chastened by sin and suffering, but they go away rejoicing, regenerated, with renewed strength and good will. We impart to them, by the power given us by Christ, pardon for the past and strength to sin no more."

"Good Sir, you are certainly claiming a wonderful power, one that cannot be easily admitted."

"Have you not read the words of Christ?" rejoined Fr. Mermillod: "'Receive ye the Holy Ghost. Whose sins you shall forgive, they are forgiven them; and whose sins you shall retain, they are retained.' (*John* 20:22-23).

"Let me give you some practical examples of this power, examples that every priest who hears Confessions meets with.

"The vast majority of those who crowd around our Confessionals are undoubtedly good-living, earnest, fervent Catholics. But at times we meet with the very wrecks of humanity, men sunk in vice for many years, weakened by repeated sins, women like Magdalen, who have fallen and been degraded. If only we can induce these poor people to come regularly to Confession and follow the very simple and practical advice we give them,

we infallibly raise them up and make them useful and trustworthy members of society."

"Confession," said another guest, "may, however,
have a very different result. If men and women
may commit sin and then run to the priest for
pardon, that is rather condoning sin—in fact, it
is **an incentive to sin**."

"You are under a grave misapprehension. No
ordinary Catholic who goes to Confession har-
bors any such idea. He knows only too well that
he cannot trifle with God. He may be able to
deceive the priest, he may even deceive himself,
but he knows full well that he cannot deceive God,
and it is God in reality who pardons, through
the instrumentality of the priest.

"Even the humblest of our faithful understand
that, to receive pardon and the consequent help
to avoid sin, they must make a sincere and firm
resolution to shun sin; they must abandon dangerous occasions of sin and strive valiantly to lead
good lives. Observing these conditions, Confession, I repeat, produces remarkable results."

THE QUESTION OF CATHOLIC CRIMINALS

"There is a little axiom, Reverend Father,"
observed the host, "which militates against your
claims: 'He who proves too much, proves nothing.' If your Confession is such a wonderful remedy
for evil, how is it that so many of your Catholics
figure among the criminals of the world? Are

there not thousands of Catholics in our prisons; do not many, too, die on the scaffold?"

This objection fell **like a bombshell** on the party. It was received with an ominous silence, and all eyes were meaningfully turned toward Fr. Mermillod, as if to ask what answer he had for that.

"I thank you," he replied, "for giving me an opportunity of making clear a most important point in our debate.

"There are thousands of Catholics who are such **merely in name**. These undoubtedly give a large number of criminals to the jails. But we do not consider these Catholics. There are, however, other thousands of Catholics who live up to their faith, who practice their religion and carry out its precepts and commands. Among these I assure you there are very few criminals. To emphasize my point still more, let me say that by real Catholics I mean those who receive the Sacraments regularly, for the Sacraments are the great founts of strength. Among these Sacraments, Confession is of the utmost importance. Catholics who confess frequently rarely or never give criminals to the prisons and murderers to the scaffold. I say *rarely*, because there are cases of sudden bursts of passion, of unexpected temptation, of violent provocation—always to be lamented, but not surprising when one considers the weakness of human nature.

"It is also certain that there are notably fewer suicides, less gross immorality among the Catholics I speak of. These statements I base not only on reliable and accurate statistics compiled by Catholics, but also on information derived from impartial Protestant sources.

"The assertion is of such great importance that I invite you all to give it your personal and honest investigation.

"For still greater clearness I will mention what might be called a third class of Catholics, men and women who seldom attend church, who practice their religion in a desultory manner, who rarely receive the Sacraments. These are lax, remiss, ignorant Catholics, who clearly belong rather to the first class, *nominal* Catholics, and cannot be looked upon as *real* Catholics."

"But, dear Sir, what can you say of so-called Catholic countries, like Spain, France, Mexico, Peru?"

"They were formerly Catholic countries. Now they are no longer so. Many Spaniards, French and Peruvians no longer deserve the name of Catholic. They are not only apostates, but they go so far as to persecute and revile the Church. However, there are still staunch Catholics among them, and to these my principle applies.

"When Judas betrayed his Lord, he could no longer be classed as an Apostle or a friend of Christ. The same applies to Catholics.

"The Jews were incontestably God's chosen people, visibly loved and protected by Him. When they fell away, as often they did, they lost all right to His protection and were most severely punished and humbled. Bad Catholics, like bad Jews, may become God's greatest enemies. As such they cannot be called the people of God nor claim the prerogatives of such.

"Our present discussion is on the merits of Confession, and my contention is that Confession, regularly practiced, makes men good Catholics, good citizens — and few if any criminals are found in their ranks."

"And may we Protestants not make with equal reason the distinction between good and bad Protestants?"

"Certainly not," replied Fr. Mermillod with a smile. "Your position is altogether different, for every Protestant has the right to think and act for himself, **yet he is still a good Protestant**.

"The more a Catholic lives up to his faith, the better a man he is; the more you act on your Protestant principles, the less good you are.

"Your principle of **private interpretation of the Scriptures** gives every one of you the right to choose for himself the doctrines he wishes to hold. The more, therefore, you act *as good Protestants*, the more you differ among yourselves and the further away you are from holding the great body of Christ's doctrine as contained in the Scriptures. Hence the appalling doctrinal differences among your various sects, among members of the same sect, and even among the members of every Protestant family — differences, observe, on important and fundamental truths. You admit or deny these doctrines as it seems well to you.

"Therefore, the more you act on your Protestant principles, the further away you are from having the whole of Christ's teaching—but, notwithstanding, **you are still good Protestants!**

"A second fundamental tenet of yours is **'Justification without works.'** The more you enforce and live up to that principle, the fewer good works you are likely to perform—and still you are all equally good Protestants!

"Really, your only chance of being good men and women is by not acting on Protestant principles! For then you are more likely to accept *all* Christ's teaching and not merely what seems good to you. Secondly, you will hold the necessity of good works, and so more readily perform them.

"I have received into the Catholic Church several excellent Protestants who assured me, after being fully instructed, that they had always believed in the doctrines of Christ contained in the Bible, without any exceptions, just as I had explained them.

"I had merely to explain to them the doctrine of Infallibility, which they not only admitted without difficulty, but declared that they had *always* had a subconscious knowledge of and virtually believed in. It was always their impression that the Church must have the fullest power to teach and insist on her teaching. These men and women did not act on Protestant principles, but were nevertheless good men and women."

WHY ALL THIS FUSS OVER SIN?

"One last objection, dear Sir," said the hostess, who, though silent during the discussion, had been one of the most intent listeners of the group.

"I fail to understand why Catholics make so much account of sins. What harm can sins do to the Almighty? Surely He does not trouble about a few wrong words or thoughts, which do harm to no one. And still my Catholic friends are horrified if our dear friends of the theater treat us to something a little fresh, or if a delightful book has a few chapters not in harmony with their way of thinking. They will not eat meat on a Friday for worlds, nor be absent from Mass though the day be cold and rainy.

"Without wishing to be offensive, I do think such fads are **prudish and smack of superstition**. We must live in the world and let live. I fully agree that crime, theft, violence are very wrong; they are sins against society."

This objection seemed also to voice the difficulty of many, judging from the interest awakened.

"Yet, dear Madam, **the sin of the Angels** was a thought of revolt, and as a result a third part of those glorious spirits lost their thrones in Heaven. It was the eating of a little fruit by our First Mother, **Eve**, that proved the undoing of the human race. Was it not an act of disobedience that deprived **Saul** of his throne, and was it not a sinful glance that led holy **David** to the commission of a heinous crime? An act of vanity, too, lost him 70,000 of his subjects. Did not the venerable **Eleazar** sacrifice his life rather than eat swine's flesh? And what about the death of **Oza** and **Ahio** for daring to touch the Ark?

"Do you forget the **Deluge**, which wiped out almost the whole human race, and the destruction of **Sodom and Gomorrha**, all because of sin?

"And in human life we see how a trifling act is construed as a great crime if it gives offense to a person in authority. How many men have given their lives in defense of their so-called honor, outraged by an imaginary insult, an incautious word, a slight. How many great men have lost their heads because of an offense to royalty— 'high treason against the King,' it was called. Sin is high treason against the King of Kings.

"Dear Madam, you fail to see that it is not the trifling act which is wrong, but the principle involved: the malice of the offense against an infinite God, to whom we owe our love, our gratitude and our allegiance.

"Surely, if God died on account of sin, sin must be dreadful. If sin is punished by Hell-fire, sin must be enormous. When you make light of sin, you judge not Catholics, but God Himself.

"A tiny drop of poison that is scarcely visible kills the strongest man; so sin, which to you seems insignificant, is an outrage to the Most High. You deplore wrongs against society, but you make nothing of sins against God!

"No one discriminates more carefully than the Catholic Church between small faults and grave faults. No one is so ready to condone trifling breaches of rule, and no one more prompt to pardon great sins, if only they are sincerely repented of, than the Catholic Church.

"To eat meat on a Friday deliberately without any reason is in reality a revolt, just as it was a revolt when Lucifer said: 'I will not serve.' Eleazar gave his life rather than eat forbidden meat.

"Evil theaters corrupt good morals; bad books are the ruin of morality and the cause of countless crimes. They are sins against society, but still more, offenses against God.

"Yes, we must live, dear Lady, in the world, but be not of the bad world. We must live and let live, as you well say, but we may not conscientiously approve or condone evil and what leads to it.

"Let me call your attention above all to the fact that the Catholic Church builds all its moral edifice on the Ten Commandments and the precepts and counsels of Christ. **She condemns nothing that Christ has not condemned**. Surely you do not maintain that the Ten Commandments and the counsels of Christ are prudish and superstitious. Yet the sins Catholics speak so much of are violations of the Commandments of God and the precepts of Christ.

"In conclusion, by sin we chase away God from us; as long as we remain in sin, we are in revolt against Him. At the same time, we surrender ourselves to the devil and give him power over us. When in sin, we are the slaves of vice and the children and slaves of Satan."

THE ACTRESS

Shortly after this last objection, all rose from the table and adjourned to a spacious salon, where they separated into small groups. Some still bombarded Fr. Mermillod with lively queries, to which he replied good-humoredly. Finally, when he was preparing to take his departure, a young actress drew him apart and said: "Father, could you possibly give me an interview tomorrow. I have something very important to say, and I think that I can explain the mystery which so happily brought you amongst us tonight. You have done incalculable good to some of us."

Fr. Mermillod readily appointed an hour to suit his fair caller and then took his leave, accompanied by his host to the automobile which had been thoughtfully placed at his disposal.

Next day, at the hour he had appointed, **Mademoiselle Blanche de Vaudois**, the young actress of the previous evening, was announced.

"Father, I am a Catholic," she explained, "one of your wandering sheep. I am a cousin of the Countess de Vaudois, and my brother and I, orphans at an early age, were educated by her with a mother's care. After my entrance into society, which was a brilliant affair, the world's pleasures and vanities proved too much for me. I was fêted and flattered and gradually lost my head. Gifted with what people called a *'divine voice,'* I resolved, in the face of all that my dear aunt and brother could say, to try my fortune on the stage. It well-nigh broke their hearts.

"Again, success awaited me. I have been the star of our company for many years. Unfortunately, I abandoned my religion almost completely, clinging to the solitary devotion of **my Rosary**, which that dear brother adjured me in his last letter, written on his deathbed, never to abandon.

"For some months my star has been declining. That young actress whose flashes of wit caused so much laughter last evening has taken my place. That I could have borne, for though hard, it is only what one must expect in our profession. Unfortunately, worse luck was in store for me. I have been almost hissed off the stage more than once. My rôle was not sympathetic, my nerves were shattered and I had not my old charm and prestige to save me. My cup was full and I had quite made up my mind last night to end it all.

"Everything was planned, I had marked the place in the lake where I intended taking the fatal plunge, a pool so deep, with banks so high, that escape was impossible. Here are three letters which I had written to dear friends begging their forgiveness.

"My doom seemed inevitably sealed, and I never dreamed that I could be dissuaded from doing what I had resolved on. I felt no fear, I was in the hands of a power greater than my own.

"Certainly, I was the sick lady you had been called to see, sick unto death. Your visitor was the spirit of my dear dead brother. Your description of him was vivid, a pen picture so clear that there can be no mistake.

"He promised in that last broken-hearted letter that he would ever pray for me before the throne of God.

"Father, he and you have saved me. I am ready to confess, if you deem me worthy of your care."

A few days after, Mademoiselle Blanche concluded her contract with the theater. She found time to visit Fr. Mermillod once more, and then left Geneva.

Less than a year after, he received a letter from a Sister Dominique of the Holy Rosary, formerly Blanche de Vaudois, from her home in a Dominican cloister, whence she assured him she had found perfect peace and where she had dedicated her *divine voice* to the glory of God.

"Use my story as you wish, good Father. It may help to save other souls like mine from irreparable ruin."

Chapter 11

THE TWO TRIBUNALS

Sometimes the thought passes through our minds, sometimes we even hear it expressed in words: "Why is God so severe?"

It will, therefore, be of interest to compare the methods followed in the administration of Divine and human justice.

In the case of **human justice**, man — weak, erring man — constitutes himself the judge of his fellowman.

A crime is committed. It is denounced immediately. The accusation is public, the sentence is severe, the punishment is rigorous.

Let us take an everyday case. Someone commits a felony, a theft, a murder. At once the minions of the law are in hot pursuit, like so many bloodhounds, on the track of the miscreant. There is no thought of secrecy, no wish to shield the culprit from shame.

The police have orders to seek him out wherever he may be found, in whatever act he may be engaged, however sacred. It may be that he is found in the midst of his hapless family, utterly unconscious of what has happened, absolutely innocent of guilt. It may be in his club among his friends, or in the public thoroughfare in the transaction of business. He is seized without warning, dragged through the streets, exposed to the gaze, the contempt, the jeers of the crowd.

Hurried before the magistrates, he is mercilessly accused, cross-examined, worried with crafty questions framed expressly to trap him into some admission of guilt. He is interrogated on matters of the strictest privacy; he is compelled to account for his every movement, to remember, and admit or deny, his every word.

The newspapers discuss the case with the utmost publicity, criticize his actions, misconstrue his motives and suggest as realities what are bare possibilities.

His family is plunged into grief, his friends shun him, suspicion lies heavy on him.

After the first phase of his martyrdom, he is left to linger for weeks or months in prison to await his trial, a prey to grief, to fear, to anxiety. His every word is noted and will be used, if possible, against him.

In the meantime, his accusers are seeking for evidence to convict him; they leave no stone unturned to secure his condemnation.

At long last the day of trial arrives. The court is filled with a crowd of curious spectators who come to amuse themselves at this scene of human suffering, to look on callously while the accused man is arraigned before his judges. On that sea of faces turned insolently upon him, no sign of sympathy is evident, no word of compassion is spoken.

The accusation is couched in such terms as to make escape difficult. Witness after witness, previously primed by the lawyers, is heard. The man's whole life is laid bare.

The evidence is set forth so artfully that it leads all to believe in his guilt. Everything that a keen, astute, accomplished barrister can urge is used against the accused. Subtle, insidious suspicions are blended with the more certain facts.

It is true there is a lawyer to defend him, but how difficult is not his task! Do what he will, he cannot shield his client from the shame, the disgrace, the ignominy of the accusations. He cannot prevent the Crown prosecutor, who is a man of keen ability, from blackening the good name, from arousing the gravest suspicion, when not absolutely certain of his client's guilt.

The accused is of course allowed to call witnesses for his defense. These are, however, bullied and harassed by a fire of cross-questions from the prosecuting lawyer, with the apparent purpose of sifting the evidence, but which have in reality the effect of nullifying whatever has been said in favor of the accused. The more effective the cross-examination, the more able the lawyer is considered to be, especially if he can make the witness unsay what he wished to say and say what he had no intention of saying. No one who has assisted at such a scene is likely to forget it, and no one who can avoid it would wish to be a witness or take part in a trial.

We must remember, too, that the man in the

dock may be innocent. It often happens at the bar of human justice that the guilty go free and the innocent are punished.

If the accused man is found guilty, the law is inexorable; it must take its course. The sentence is crushing; the convicted man's honor is blasted forever. His wife and innocent children share in his eternal disgrace. There is no hope that the black cloud will rise; they will be forever known as the wife of a felon, the children of a murderer.

Such is the procedure of human tribunals where men accuse, judge, convict and condemn men like themselves.

But it is all necessary, so they say. Society must be saved. The wicked must be punished. Order must be maintained.

We do not contest the good intentions of the court, nor do we deny the necessity of upholding order. We merely bewail the necessity, if necessity there be, for such cruel measures.

Nor is our picture overdrawn. We are describing cases of everyday occurrence as published by the world's press.

But is there no appeal? No redress? Yes, but the costs of the case in the first instance were enormous. In case of an appeal, they might be overwhelming, and the issue is at best doubtful.

HOW GOD ADMINISTERS JUSTICE

Now let us see how **Divine Justice** is administered by the Great God of Heaven to His sinful and rebellious creatures.

He calls the guilty one aside secretly by the voice of conscience, heard by none but the sinner himself, so that no one is made aware of his guilt.

He leads him to a hidden place where no one accuses him. No witnesses are called to give testimony against him. His soul may be black with guilt, he may have outraged his Maker, but here no one may scorn him. He kneels at the feet of a loving Father, who is there to speak to him, not of punishment, but of forgiveness, who reminds him not of God's Justice but of God's Mercy, and finally who assures him of God's complete and entire pardon.

There is no thought of a death penalty, no threat of long years of imprisonment, no fear of perpetual disgrace.

He himself confesses his faults; he is believed, no doubts are cast on the truth of his words. The minister of God fills his soul with comfort, his heart with peace, his will with strength. He applies to the sinful soul, soiled and degraded by sin, the Precious Blood of Jesus, which removes its stains and makes the guilty man a sight that Angels love to look upon.

A light penance is imposed, which the absolved sinner gladly fulfills. He receives valuable advice, which he puts faithfully into practice. He comes back from time to time and gets fresh comfort, fresh strength and new graces.

There are no costs, no fines, no expenses!

The accused rises up repentant, God's love sweetening his sorrow, God's mercy filling him with gratitude, God's grace giving him strength to sin no more.

Here indeed God's promise is fulfilled: "If your sins be as scarlet, they shall be made as white as snow." (*Isaias* 1:18).

BUT "GOD IS NOT MOCKED."

Yes, the Almighty is infinitely patient with His wayward, sinful children. They are weak. He is fully aware of their weaknesses, but He offers them such strength, such grace, such help that whatever sin they have committed, they must confess it as being fully and entirely due to their own deliberate fault.

They are blind? He throws light on their soul. He makes them see the black ingratitude, the malice of sin. It is not as if they had sinned without knowing it.

They are listless, indifferent, apathetic? He rouses them from their lethargy by allowing them to see the deaths, the punishments of others.

They are absorbed by business, by pleasures?

He is constantly calling them by the voice of conscience, showing them the dangers they run, offering them wonderful rewards if they are good.

What does He ask them to do? Nothing difficult, nothing hard, especially if they will only use the graces and aids He offers them.

These aids are, firstly, to ask Him by prayer for help. In return, He promises to give them everything they require. What could be easier?

Secondly, He counsels them to apply His Precious Blood to their souls by frequent Confession. Then they will triumph over all difficulties.

Thirdly, He invites them to receive Him often in the Blessed Eucharist, with all the graces He then bestows.

What could be more delightful than to receive the God of infinite sweetness and mercy and love into their souls? But what does He ask them to do?

Simply to act as good sons to the best of Fathers, to do their duty, to fulfill their obligations. He asks them to be just and upright and pure; not to steal nor kill nor do evil. In a word, He bids them be honest, respectable men and women, not criminals, nor lawbreakers. Could He do more for us? Could He ask less of us?

This infinite patience of God endures until the last moment of life. Only when His Goodness is despised, His mercy abused and His love outraged, does **His Justice** claim its part. God by His essence is just, and sin in its essence is evil and has to be punished. But first God exhausts all the resources of **His Mercy,** which is above all His works, to avoid, if possible, using His Justice. ("The Lord is sweet to all: and his tender mercies are over all his works."—*Ps.* 144:9.)

Then, if of our own free will we rebel and continue to rebel, we finally bring the thunders of

His Justice upon our heads. His Justice must punish obstinate sin.

Many of those who ridicule Confession during life change their minds as death approaches and seek, alas in vain, for the consolation they had for so many years scorned.

D'Alembert wished to be reconciled with God on his deathbed, but Condorcet, his false friend, saw to it that the priest could not get access to the dying man, and so he died a prey to bitter remorse and appalling fears.

Diderot showed signs of repentance and had even spoken a few times with a priest. His friends, alarmed at his change of views and fearful lest his conversion might bring ridicule upon their philosophy, hurried him away to the country where the priest could not visit him.

Voltaire, in the last days of his life, sought for the consolation of Confession, but once again cruel, cynical friends denied him this supreme consolation. And it is said that he died in despair. He had never been sincere in his attacks on religion, and he came to know, when it was too late, that "God is not mocked." (*Gal.* 6:7).

We leave our readers to decide whether the Good God is severe.

Chapter 12

JESUS AND SINNERS

In the sublime pages of our Saviour's life there is nothing so touching as His sweet condescension with sinners, and what is much to our purpose, Our Lord still continues this ministry of love and mercy in our regard.

He tells us that the countless sins which bring calamity and ruin upon the human race flow from three great sources: the World, the Flesh and the Devil.

The Flesh with its vile sensuality, its soft blandishments, its subtle attractions, its gross pleasures, precipitates vast multitudes into Hell.

The World with its frivolities, its false principles, its pride and lust of gain, draws countless souls from God.

The Devil, who is unheeded by many, and by others treated as a myth about one who does not exist, is a very great and dangerous reality. Filled with implacable hate against God and against us who are destined to replace him in Heaven, he is going about, as St. Peter tells us, **like a roaring lion**, seeking whom he may devour. (Cf. *1 Ptr.* 5:8). St. Paul in his turn warns us that we are not fighting with men of flesh and blood like ourselves

but with the Principalities and Powers of dark-
ness (cf. *Eph.* 6:12), fallen angels who still possess
all their wondrous intelligence, but which they
now use to bring about our ruin.

THE ADULTERESS

One day when Jesus was teaching in the Tem-
ple, the Scribes and Pharisees dragged into His
presence an unfortunate woman taken in the commission of the hateful sin of adultery.

Among the Jews this sin was looked upon as
the most shameful of crimes and punished with
pitiless severity. Even the nearest and dearest rela-
tives of the guilty woman were held to denounce
her, and then both she and her accomplice were
publicly stoned to death.

The unfortunate creature taken by the
Pharisees, fearing with good reason the awful fate
that awaited her, trembled in every limb and hung
her head in shame, trying to hide her face, pale
as death, from the contemptuous gaze of the
crowd. Her brutal captors thrust her roughly into
the presence of Jesus, denouncing her crime and
demanding of Him what they should do with her,
hoping that He would condemn her without
mercy. She dared not defend herself; she was guilty
and could not hope for pardon, nay, she even
feared to look into the face of Him who was to
judge her.

Our sweet Lord looked at the sinner with
infinite pity as she stood before Him overpow-

ered with shame and terror. He showed no sign of contempt, not even of anger. He did not draw back a single step; He feared no defilement.

Slowly He turned His eyes so full of compassion from the woman and, with an air of majesty, confronted the angry rabble. At once twenty voices were raised clamoring for the woman's death, twenty voices of human tigers thirsting for blood.

Jesus gazed on them unmoved, noted the relentless hate that blazed in their eyes and saw the hidden depths of malice of their hearts, cloaked over by the pretense of zeal.

With a gesture of authority He compelled their silence. Every ear was strained to hear the words of condemnation!

Clearly and distinctly the voice of the Master rang out: "He that is without sin among you, let him first cast a stone at her."

Dismayed, confounded by the unexpected sentence, the Pharisees and their satellites slowly slunk away, discomfited and reproved, leaving Jesus alone with the sinner.

Then Jesus said to her: "Woman, where are they that accused thee? Hath no man condemned thee?"

And she replied: "No man, Lord."

And Jesus said: "Neither will I condemn thee. Go, and now sin no more." (*John* 8:11).

Who could paint a picture more sublime or imagine a scene more divine in its mercy, more human and consoling in its loving tenderness?

The sinful woman, no longer trembling, looked into the face of the Lord with boundless gratitude and love.

She spoke no word of thanks. What could she say? When the heart is full, words fail to express our feelings: silence is best. The eyes, though, are eloquent, and Jesus saw in the eyes of the woman such love as a seraph might envy.

An immense wave of relief passed over her soul. She was safe, saved from an awful death from which, a few moments before, she had seen no escape. Still, that was not the thought now uppermost in her mind.

She only thought of the infinite compassion of the Divine Rabbi who had defended her against her enemies.

The accents of His voice were still sounding in her ears; they would sound there for all time.

"Go, and now sin no more."

No, no, nevermore would she sin again. Her love, her loyalty she had given to this Lord, and that love she would never withdraw.

THE WORLD'S GREATEST SCOURGE

The sin of adultery was considered at all times a most grievous crime, and the penalties decreed against it were exceedingly severe.

The Romans, like the Jews, stoned the guilty parties to death. The Greeks punished adultery with the same awful rigors as parricide.

The Mohammedans buried the adulterous woman up to her waist and then stoned her mercilessly to death.

The Britons burned her alive and hanged her accomplice over her ashes. The more barbarous nations used torments still more cruel, the very mention of which makes one shudder.

Too, the woman was always looked upon as the greater delinquent, and the laws were especially severe in her regard.

This consensus of opinion is a certain proof of how enormous the sin has been considered by mankind in general.

It was left to Christianity to see that a more even justice was meted out to the woman.

Adultery is without any doubt a crime that cries to Heaven for vengeance—and not only adultery, but **impurity** in its every form, whether in thought, word or deed.

It is today the world's greatest scourge.

TWO GREAT CAUSES OF IMPURITY

Therefore, it is of importance to study the principal causes of the devastating spread of this awful evil.

Broadly speaking, there are two great causes, namely, ignorance of the deplorable results of the vice, on the one hand, and lack of moral training and practical religion, on the other.

Some allege that the vice is due to climatic conditions and is more prevalent in warm countries. This can scarcely be correct, for the evil is fully as appalling in some of the northern and cold climates.

Others maintain that it is due to the decadence of race. Quite the contrary is the fact; the decadence of a race is due to the prevalence of these abuses, and once this vice is cured, the race regains its pristine health and energy.

The problem has received much attention and it can be safely held that the first great cause of the plague of impurity is the gross ignorance existing of its malice, of the awful punishments attached to it, and of the fatal consequences which attend its practice. While people live in blank ignorance of the evils of which we have just been speaking, there are thousands of temptations — attractive, insidious, seductive, inviting — almost compelling men and women to the commission of sin.

The old horror of adultery has in great part disappeared, popular opinion is no longer so strong against it. The number of divorces, the facility of obtaining them, the paltry reasons put forward as a just motive for them, the little importance attached to the stability of family life, are nothing else than a public sanction of adultery. Then there is a wild, uncontrolled love of pleasure which leads to an infinity of abuses.

Women, too, have lost respect for themselves and all love of feminine virtues.

Thus it is that impurity in all its forms is rampant all the world over.

MOVIE THEATERS, DENS OF IMMORALITY

Witness the grossness and sensuousness of the movie theaters, where, as a matter of course, men take their wives, where mothers take their daughters, where even young children are taken by their foolish parents for amusement!

These theaters are dens of immorality, schools of vice, where sin is popularized, legalized and taught in the most shameless and effective way.

There boys are taught to steal, to admire daring robbery, to imitate it. Even murder is made light of.

Indecency in its every form is made popular. Girls and boys, young men and women look at the most shameful films with the greatest complacency.

Is it any wonder that young married men and women insensibly put into practice what they are every day looking at and drinking in?

Some months ago an American Bishop and his ecclesiastical censors were invited to give their opinion of some films. They were utterly astonished at what was shown them and declared their horror of it all. They found it incredible that any film magnate could think of showing such filthy productions to the public.

Yet the persons most surprised at the result of the exhibition were the film magnates, who protested vehemently that their films were true to nature and exactly what people wanted and what filled the theaters!

The Bishops, in the face of such an idea, united and protested, with the result that **80 million dollars worth** of abominable films were condemned and withdrawn.

Yet these are the shows which young wives, boys and girls and children are allowed to watch, with the full consent of their parents.*

Libraries and bookstalls are flooded with immoral literature. Vile novels, disgraceful pictures, which stimulate the worst passions, are for sale everywhere.

Mark, too, the fashions, which show the lack of even the sense of modesty: the pagan dress or scandalous lack of dress on the beaches, on board ships and in public places. Young girls are the most barefaced sinners; they seem to have lost all comprehension and feeling of purity.

It is often said that a wicked cow is far more dangerous than a ferocious bull, and that the lioness is more vicious and savage than the lion.

Women, too, when they lose their self-respect and self-control, become most depraved and despicable. How can sensible men take such women for wives? How can they trust them? And if these women marry, what kind of mothers will they be?

---

*All this obviously applies even more today. Moreover, shameful shows have invaded the very sanctuary of the home through television and videos.—*Editor*, 1992.

THE GREAT CULPRITS

It has been well said that the great culprits of the present day are **fathers and mothers** who bring up their children in the gravest ignorance of the dangers before them, dangers that they cannot possibly avoid and into which they will infallibly fall if not duly warned.*

They allege that they dare not rob their children of innocence.

Whoever dared ask them to do so?

But this is exactly what they are doing. They are deliberately hiding the precipice over which the children are bound to plunge headlong.

They keep them in ignorance of the most elementary and essential facts of life, facts which must be known sooner or later.

Now if these facts are not prudently but clearly explained while there is yet time, a morbid curiosity is aroused in the child's mind. This is increased by conversation and contact with other children, with servants, with bad companions.

It is whetted by immoral conversations, by lewd pictures and illustrations, by immoral reading, by visits to places of amusement, until sensuality has gotten a thorough grasp of the mind, and bad instincts—which are extremely difficult to

---

*This applies today more than ever, with the additional warning that parents are obligated to see that their children are not subjected to the corrupting influence of classroom "sex education."—*Editor*, 1992.

remove—have been formed in the heart.

Now, had careful, clean, but very forcible instructions been imparted by fathers and mothers, all these dangers would have been avoided, or at least been lessened by ninety-nine percent.

Such wise explanations, far from being detrimental, inspire disgust for the vice and fill boys and girls with a real fear of its terrific results. Moreover, they go far to allay the cravings of passion and self-indulgence.

Impurity is an evil that attacks equally the individual, the family, society and the nation. It is, as we have said, the great curse of humanity and the real cause of much of the moral degradation and decadence noticeable in some of the great nations of modern times.

FACTS, FACTS, FACTS

Here are facts which should be thoroughly explained to every boy and girl.

The ablest physicians, Catholics and non-Catholics, do not hesitate to say that men and women habitually addicted to sins of impurity, even though it be only in thought, lose all dignity, self-control and will power.*

---

*In this regard we may note the "coincidence" that work habits and scholastic discipline have degenerated in our world now that sexual "fantasizing" and solitary sins of impurity (both are mortal sins) are considered "normal."—*Editor*, 1992.

Their sense of honor and duty disappears. The sensual man or woman is capable of the basest treachery and is utterly unworthy of confidence.

Worse still, eminent specialists affirm that many of the worst forms of melancholy, neurasthenia and even madness* are due to the practice of this degrading sin.

In addition to mental maladies, which are sufficient to fill us with terror, this hateful vice begets the most loathsome forms of bodily disease. The most salutary lesson one could learn would be to visit a hospital especially set aside for these dreadful maladies, painful and disgusting in the extreme. The sight would drive terror into the most reckless.

Now, what is appalling is that in some countries there are as many as 750 of every 1,000 inhabitants victims, in various degrees, of these awful sicknesses, persons who have become depraved, enervated, utter wrecks.

These 750 depraved victims of vice are husbands and sons, businessmen and professional men, and naturally their ideas and example affect the sound minds of the other 250.

It follows as a matter of course that such men are devoid of character, are weak, unstable, morally unfit.

---

*Today these disorders would be called *neurosis* and *psychosis.—Editor,* 1992.

No wonder that in such nations it is difficult to find sound governing bodies imbued with the spirit of patriotism, self-sacrifice and rectitude, so absolutely necessary for the nation's welfare.

The percentage of victims in countries where the conditions are equal but where precautions are taken against the spread of vice is one per thousand. What a difference: **750** in 1,000, and **1** in 1,000!

That explains the splendid mental activity and excellent *morale* that animates some nations and the decadence that prevails in others.

GOD STRIKES THE IMPURE

Terrible as the natural consequences are, much more to be feared are the punishments of God.

1. Countless souls are every day being precipitated into Hell because of the sin of impurity, even by sins of impure thought. Some holy writers do not hesitate to say that this sin of itself sends a hundred times more souls to Hell than all the other sins together.

2. Every sin of impurity carries with it terrible chastisement. It would be easier for a thief to commit a robbery under the very eyes of a policeman and escape than for a man to commit a sin of impurity and not be punished. God sees, and God exacts the penalty.

3. The most awful temporal punishments fall on those who thus sin. The curse falls on the individual, on society, and on the country where the sins are committed. The Deluge destroyed the whole human race, excepting eight persons, because of impurity.

God rained down fire from Heaven which consumed Sodom and Gomorrha because of impurity.

How terrible must be this sin to provoke such chastisement from so good and merciful a God!

Ever since these two cases, the most appalling calamities have overtaken cities and towns where this vile sin is practiced. Not only the great Saints, but missionaries and other priests who have long experience with souls, can tell of the deaths, sudden and terrible, of those addicted to impurity. How many boys and girls, men and women, have been struck dead in the very commission of the sin!

Impurity is the **great cause** of suffering in the world, and people just will not see it! **Ignorance** and **forgetfulness** of these facts bring untold misery and are the cause of perdition to innumerable souls.

THE SNAKE IN THE GRASS

There is another point that calls for attention. It is that this loathsome vice appears so natural. The devil conceals it, especially its beginnings, under the cloak of friendship and affection. It is just like a cancer. It lies concealed until it has taken deep roots and is then very difficult to cure.

This is another reason why all the dreadful consequences, natural and supernatural, should be clearly, strongly, unceasingly dinned into the heads of the young. Doctors are using all their efforts to prevent tuberculosis rather than to cure it. Such action is far wiser and more efficacious. Prevention is decidedly better than cure. The same principle applies, but with a thousand times more reason, to the prevention of impurity. It is easy to prevent it; it is most difficult to cure it.

Many wise and experienced teachers think — and with the greatest reason — that 90% of sin could be prevented and the greatest horror of the vice instilled into the minds of the young by proper education.

Parents, doctors and teachers could do an immense amount to stem the awful tide of this corruption.

CONFESSION AN INFALLIBLE CURE

Practicing Catholics have, of course, no excuse. They have the divine remedy given by Jesus Christ. He saw more clearly than all others the havoc wrought by sins of the flesh and, in the plenitude of His Mercy and Love, gave us a most efficacious cure for them.

Confession can cure all sins, but it has a most especial power in eradicating impurity, in healing weak fallen nature and in restoring to man his native strength and purity.

One can never repeat too often that Confession was given not only to pardon sin, but to cure it, to drag it out by the roots from the soul.

Experienced priests see this every day of their lives. Let the most abandoned sinner come to them, a man or woman sunk in vice, surrounded by temptations; if only the priest can get these poor weaklings to come **frequently** to the Sacraments, he will soon have the satisfaction of seeing them thoroughly and entirely regenerated.

Therefore, frequent Confession — **weekly Confession** — is the great bulwark against sin!

Priests can never insist too much with their penitents, young and old, on the necessity of going to weekly Confession.

Mothers and fathers, and teachers of every kind, should do everything in their power to induce children to make a lifelong practice of frequent Confession.

Many Catholic doctors have the greatest confidence in the efficacy of this Sacrament and recommend it to their patients and friends, and it is a pity that all doctors do not see their way to do the same.

The writer has conferred with many experienced confessors, and all, without exception, agree that no vice is so gross, so deep-rooted, so vicious that it will not yield to frequent Confession — all the more so since, after Confession, the penitents receive God Himself in Holy Communion.

*Appendix**

HOW TO GO TO CONFESSION

Examine your conscience.

Be sorry for your sins and make up your mind not to sin again (at least not to commit mortal sin again).

(Kneel down, make the Sign of the Cross and say. . .)

"Bless me, Father, for I have sinned. It has been _____ days (weeks, months, years) since my last Confession. I said my penance and received Holy Communion. I confess to Almighty God and to you, Father, that I have. . ."

(Here tell all the mortal sins you may have committed since your last good Confession, and the number of times you committed them, and then, if possible, tell the number and kind of your venial sins. Then say. . .)

"I am sorry for these and all the sins of my past life, and I ask pardon of God and penance of you, Father."

---

*Added by the Publisher to the 1992 edition.

(Listen to what the priest says, and especially note the penance he gives you. Then say an Act of Contrition.)

The priest will give you absolution and finish by saying words such as, "God bless you. Go in peace."

After leaving the confessional, say or perform the penance the priest assigned you.

ACT OF CONTRITION

O MY GOD, I am heartily sorry for having offended Thee. And I detest all my sins because I dread the loss of Heaven and the pains of Hell; but most of all because they offend Thee, my God, who art all good and deserving of all my love. I firmly resolve, with the help of Thy grace, to confess my sins, to do penance, and to amend my life. Amen.

If you have enjoyed this book, consider making your next selection from among the following . . .